God's Precious Daughters, Leave The Spirit Of Vanity, Return Back to Him

Turn Back to God

JACQUELINE GREENE

authorHOUSE®

AuthorHouse™
1663 Liberty Drive
Bloomington, IN 47403
www.authorhouse.com
Phone: 1 (800) 839-8640

Published by AuthorHouse 05/28/2020

ISBN: 978-1-7283-6294-6 (sc)
ISBN: 978-1-7283-6293-9 (e)

Print information available on the last page.

Contents

Chapter 1

Image problem

Let's face it, we all have struggled with our image from childhood, into our adulthood. We all want to look as beautiful as we possibly can to attract others to ourselves. We have found different methods to use to beautify ourselves, because we do not like the image we see in the mirror. We may have questioned ourselves "why I look the way I look or why I look like my mother or my father." I know, I used to feel the same way. When others said me, "you look like your mother, or you look like your father," I would tell them, "look like myself." It used to irritate me to no end that someone would say I looked like my parents.

Guess what? I look like my parents.

I have accepted the fact that's the reason God chose my Parents to bring into form all the features of my exist for His purpose. The beautiful thing about being in Christ, He takes the ugliness of the flesh and gives us the beauty of the spirit. Because we are unable to see our spirit and see its beauty, we continue to try to improve the flesh.

It was hard for me to embrace the girl in the mirror. I thought she was ugly and didn't have what it took to survive in a mean cruel world. I was always teased and bullied growing up!

I didn't know at the time I was made in God's image and likeness.

Genesis 1:27 KJV *So God created man in his own image, in the image of God created him; male and female created him them.*

In Genesis 1:26-27 KJV the truth is declared that God created man in His own" image after His likeness. The two ideas denote the resemblance to God. We can conclude that we are made in God's Image and likeness. You may ask "okay, what do that look like?" It looks like God's spoken Word concerning you. The real beauty comes from within you. It is more about your inner soul and spirit than your outer flesh.

If you are a bible reader, you will come to understand the importance of your soul and spirit rather than your physical appearance. The reason is that our physical lives are temporal. It has an expiration date. When you feel beautiful inside, it will help you to present it on the outside to those around.

So, as you can see, you are made in the image of our Creator. When you are a child, you have no recollection of why you are here. You are not focusing on the spiritual, but the natural. The reason for this is because of our environment, we are in the natural world, looking at the flesh of ourselves and others. That's the reason we have always compared ourselves with others.

If you have noticed, some of us who have curly hair want straight hair, then if we have straight hair, we want curly hair. We are a people that is never satisfied. Let's not talk about skin color. God wants us to appreciate and embrace what He has designed and created for His Glory. You are His Bride, so He created you the way He wanted you to be. It's not about color, hair, and sizes; it's about God designing you for purpose to bring Him Glory.

The way someone else's viewed us is the way we have looked at ourselves. In our adulthood, if someone calls us a name that was not given to us by our parents, we adjust to it and own it. Why? Because as a human being, we want love and acceptance. We look for man to affirm us in the way we look, think, and act.

We have been driven by man, that it's unbearable, to agree with our Creator.

The Lord is saying, your image problem is the way you view yourself, and not accepting the fact that He made you in His image and likeness. God wanted us to duplicate Him, He wanted us to appreciate what He has created through His hands. He wanted us to enjoy Him as our creator. He was so delighted in making man for His purpose, that He gave man a Helpmate, to subdue the land. But the disobedience of the first family fell on all mankind. Let take a look at this account: ***Genesis 3: 3-7*** KJV

***3** But of the fruit of the tree, which is in the midst of the garden, God hath said, Ye shall not eat of it, neither shall ye touch it, lest ye die. **4** And the serpent said unto the woman, Ye shall not surely die: **5** For God doth know that in the day ye eat thereof, then your eyes shall be opened, and ye shall be as gods, knowing good and evil. **6** And when the woman saw that the tree was good for food, and that it was pleasant to the eyes, and a tree to be desired to make one wise, she took of the fruit thereof, and did eat, and gave also unto her husband with her; and he did eat and the eyes of them both were opened, and they knew that they were naked; and they sewed fig leaves together and made themselves aprons.*

Did you see what happened? Adam and Eve were not concerned about how they looked until they were exposed for their disobedience. They really had it made, until they decided to take the advice of a snake. Did you know that in today's times, Men and Women are continuing listening to a snake, and not being aware of it? In reading the above scripture, we can see that God had provided them food from the other trees in the garden, then, here comes Satan a snake, twisted the words of God, and allow Eve to lust with her eyes the tree that the lord told them not to partake. Satan, told Eve, the day you eat of it, you will be like gods. Adam and Eve, knew the different of the tree that they were not to touch, however, they disobey God, and took the advice from the snake, and sinned against God. At that point, they fully understood the nature of being evil. When Adam and Eve lost their place of innocence, they understood the evil nature was presence within them. Satan knew that if he could persuade them to eat of the tree, it will open their eyes to know good and evil, What the enemy didn't say, that by them knowing good and evil, it will damage their relationship with God. (How did knowledge of good and evil make man like God? Genesis 3:22 KJV www. Gotquestions.org)

We are so focused on who likes us or who doesn't. We forget that our loving Savior loves us unconditionally. We forget that it's His Love for us that keeps us. We forget that no one would ever love us, the way He does. Our Savior died for us. He took what was lost and marred and restored it back.

We can see here that Adam and Eve had it made, they didn't have to make their own way, they had their God and their Creator providing all their needs. But they decided to take matters into their own hands. Isn't that just like us, taking matters into our own hands? We want to make our own way. God wants us to return our hearts back to Him so we can know who we really are in Him. He created us the way He saw fit, and what we have done is listened to a snake, that's right! who told us that we were not beautiful enough. Then we go out and get different things to adorn our flesh to look like Hollywood stars.

We are so prone to feeling negative about ourselves. When the pressures of life approach us, we are unable to handle its challenges. It sends us into a downward spiral effect. Living in a low-esteem of yourself will causes many other problems in your life. There is help, if you need to talk to someone about feeling bad about yourself image. Don't allow the pressures of life and the bullying of others to take you out of who you really are.

So, how can I get rid of this image that has distorted my view of myself? It will come when you totally commit your way to the Lord Psalms 37:5 *commit thy way unto the Lord; trust also in Him; and He shall bring it to pass.* You must commit to Him, and Love on Him and stay in His presence, then you will not continue to see yourself with an image problem, but you will see the Lord shining on you. You will be able to love yourself the way God loves you.

Don't let your past mistake take advantage over you and keep you in a place of shame but allow your past to be the past as you continue to move forward in the things of God. The past is there, where you learned from your errors, you learned through life's experiences and consequences. When you gain that knowledge of loving God and loving yourself, then that's when your image problem will no longer hunt you down. You will be able to appreciate the masterpiece that the Lord God has created.

Psalm 139:14 KJV *tells us that we are* **fearfully** *and* **wonderfully** *made,* **Marvelous** *are your works, and that my soul knows very well.*

Fearfully is **yare'** in Hebrew that means to fear, be afraid, 2 to stand in awe of, be awed, 3 to fear, reverence, honor, respect

Wonderfully is Palah in Hebrew that means to be distinct, marked out, be separated, be distinguished, 2 to be wonderful, 3 to make separate, set apart

Marvelous is **Pala** in Hebrew that means be surpassing, be extraordinary, separate by distinguishing action. It is also to be beyond one's power, be extraordinary Psalm 104:24 KJV O Lord, how **manifold** are your works! In **wisdom** have you made them all; the earth is full of your creatures.

Manifold is **rabab** in Hebrew that means to be or become many, or become much, be or become great.

Wisdom is **chokmah** in Hebrew that means skill, shrewdness, prudence.

As we can see, our creator formed us out of His wisdom and determined our likeness according to His will. We are made in His image and likeness, guess what? We have His DNA. Our parents were the instrument that was used to give us the varieties of things that we needed to be in the earth realm. We all come from God who created us. He wants us to see ourselves, as He sees us, and appreciate His handiwork. Amen.

We serve an Amazing God who desires our love and affection. He has given His love unto us His creation. The Lord has purposed us for His design and to do His will on the earth. He wants us to follow His leading by the Holy Spirit and to focus on the task at hand.

The task at hand is to Love the Lord our God with all our heart, mind and soul and love our neighbor as ourselves. If we love ourselves, we are instructed to love our neighbors as ourselves. Let's leave the image to our creator, who is designing us for purpose.

Let's appreciate who we are in His eyes only. Let us love what our Heavenly Father has created for His purpose. Turn our true attention to Him and be alright with the image that we see in the mirror. Tell our Lord that you love Him and what He has designed in you. Don't continue getting caught up in the webs of Satan, about your looks. Appreciate Your God and Glorify Him.

When we allow our Father in heaven to take care our image problem, it will allow us to focus on the matter at hand for Him. When we appreciate our color, our hair, and our body features, it will give us the satisfaction of relying on our creator to continue the masterpiece that He is developing. We are able to rest in His handiwork and begin to be amazed at what He is designing within us. To rid ourselves of our image problem will be to trust what He develops.

Chapter 2

Take off the Mask

In this chapter, the issue is as believers, like to put on a mask to disguise flaws within. We want people to be fooled to think of ourselves as someone we are not. The reason that we feel the way we feel is we need to connect to the Lord Jesus to find out our identity. Our identity lies in knowing Him. If we don't know Christ, we will have a problem in knowing our true self.

We think people won't love us if they know what we're really like.

Childhood experience conditions us to fear rejection as adults. On the other hand, if we feel our parents' love is conditional, we might carry into our adult relationships the fear that others will reject us if they find out we are "unworthy." So, we continue to pretend with them.

We're afraid people will think we're not good enough, to measure up to their expectations. They will wonder how I can be a good person and still have serious struggles. I'm afraid they will think I'm a hypocrite and a liar if I still have those things in my life that is keeping me down.

We may think people really don't care about us. Even when they ask us "How are you doing?" we perceive they are asking out of politeness and not because they want to know. So, we smile and answer, "Fine," We have trouble believing anyone is really interested in us. We're so afraid of or what others may say about us in a form of gossip. Today, the Lord is saying release and put down the mask. I am here to rescue you from the expectations of men. Put down your mask and present who you are for those around you to be able to see the real you. I will give them the heart to see you the way I see you. Stop pretending and allow Me your Savior, to present you whole.

As believers we must be in a need of deep cleansing from the Holy Spirit. We must ask the Holy Spirit to Psalm 139:23-24 KJV "Search me, O God, and know my Heart; see if there is any wicked way in me." There is a need to seek God for all preventative measures. David realized that He needed God to show him if there was anything offensive in his heart towards God. His desire was to allow the Holy Spirit to go beneath the surface of his problem. He wanted the deep things in his heart to be known and give all of it to God in repentance. Proverbs 4:23 teaching about guarding his heart. This is a time in your life when you can ask the Lord to cleanse your heart. You are giving the Holy Spirit to go deep into the issues of your heart. 1 Corinthians 2:10 KJV "For the Spirit searches all things, yes, the deep things of God." When we seek and search God's Word, His Alive and Active Word gets into your heart and cleanse it from all fleshly thoughts or desires.

You must ask the Lord to take you back into the muddy place of your life to discover the depths of the hurts that need to be healed by the Word of God. Sometimes we must go deeper and allow the Spirit of God to do a deep cleaning. When you take off the old man it will give you a more beautiful glow. And then you're ready to be used for the Master use. In this hour that each one of us are in, The Lord Jesus desires for us to embrace Him more than this temporal world. Jesus wants us to desire to be beautiful in our soul. Why? Because it's the soul man that goes on with the spirit. If we allow the Lord to show us the way spiritually, then we can see no need for a mask. You and I will have no desire to wear a mask. But with the help of the Holy Spirit we will be able to desire Jesus.

He is the true beauty in this temporal world. When you can look to Jesus, then you are able to see your real beauty.

It is truly God's pleasure and purpose for us to allow Him to wash us clean and to be glowing. Without spot, wrinkle, or blemish. He sent His Son, Jesus, for that very purpose. If the mask you are applying is for prevention of hurts and pain from others. then pray, keep your heart open and your ears attentive to the Holy Spirit. Let the Holy Spirit shine on you and remove all that you need to see your real beauty.

Ephesians 4;22-24 AMP

22 Strip yourselves of your former nature [put off and discard your old unrenewed self-] which characterized your previous manner of life and becomes corrupt through lusts *and* desires that spring from delusion; **23** And be constantly renewed in the spirit of your mind [having a fresh mental and spiritual attitude], **24**

And put on the new nature (the regenerate self) created in God's image, [Godlike] in true righteousness and holiness.

Paul is saying to each one of us, that we must take off the old nature, our lust for our flesh. Those things that we desire to look good. All those things are only vanity. It holds no real value. We are mere dust in the earth. When we leave this temporal place, we will return to dust. Just like the dirt we walk upon on this earth.

The real beauty comes from within. If we will allow the Holy Spirit to cleanse up with His word, then we will be beautiful inside and out. Don't allow man to dictate to you your worth or your beauty. Take off the mask of your pain, allow the Holy Spirit to do a major cleansing in you.

Colossians 3:8 AMP *But now put away and rid yourselves [completely] of all these things: anger, rage, bad feeling toward others,* *curses and slander, and foulmouthed abuse and shameful utterances from your lips! 9 Do not lie to one another, for you have stripped off the old (unregenerate) self with its evil practices,*

10 And have clothed yourselves with the new [spiritual self-], which is [ever in the process of being] renewed and remolded into [fuller and more perfect [b]knowledge upon] knowledge after the image (the likeness) of Him Who created it.

Ask the Lord to help you in those areas that are not pleasing to Him. Ask him to help you to get rid of those things that keep you confined to its lust. Ask the Lord to purify you for His use in this earthly body. We all need help from the Lord to rid those things of this world that we lust for unaware. We all want to argue about whether God approves of our made-up selves or our natural looks. This topic is very controversial, because there are those that say it doesn't matter. Whether you agree or not; what matters to Jesus is your inner man, your soul man. That is so important to Him.

Looking here in the scripture is saying do not lie. Putting on a mask is a lie. So, rid yourselves of all your practices that disqualifies you to do the work for your Master Jesus. Let His design of you to be enough for you to embrace and find the real you. It's not what man thinks but what Jesus thinks. Instead of getting upset about this topic, seek God's face on what He really thinks. It's truly about Souls. Our ministry is not based on how we look, but what we are doing for the Kingdom of God.

Colossians 3:12AMP

12 Clothe yourselves therefore, as God's own chosen ones (His own picked representatives), [who are] purified and holy and well-beloved [by God Himself, by putting on behavior marked by] tenderhearted pity and mercy, kind feeling, a lowly opinion of yourselves, gentle ways, [and] patience [which is tireless and long-suffering, and has the power to endure whatever comes, with good temper].

Paul is reminding us what we need to do to take off our masks. We are the Bride of Christ; we must be dressed for purification and holiness. We must desire humility and be disciplined in the working of the Holy Spirit. We must remember that we are the temple of the Holy Spirit. The Lord purifies us through His Word. He invests in us by refining us in holiness. He purifies us in setting us apart from the ideologies of man. He gives us purpose to achieve real beauty found in Him.

If we desire our real beauty to shine and look good before others, it is to put the applications of the Word to be deemed holy unto our God.

Colossians 3:13 Amp *Be gentle and forbearing with one another and, if one has a difference (a grievance or complaint) against another, readily pardoning each other; even as the Lord has [freely] forgiven you, so must you also [forgive].* **14**

And above all these [put on] love and enfold yourselves with the bond of perfectness [which binds everything together completely in ideal harmony].

This verse is the beauty of the spirit of God. We must put on love and compassion to those who will walk on our path of life. If we need body enhancements, let's wear love, peace, joy, longsuffering, gentleness, kindness, meekness, faithfulness and self-control. (Galatians 5:22-23 AMP) Let's wear them well. Beauty is truly deeper than the surface of our external existence. When you have the application of Jesus, it will bring to the forefront the pure essences of beauty.

Life is difficult enough without the added stress of frantically camouflaging our weaknesses. But why is it so important to be honest with each other? When we unmask, it helps others that we are in relationship with, to see us in the real light of who we are. It helps us to have a desire to live in the realness of God as His created being. We, will be able to unmask to show all those who may be on our path, that you are who God created. we will no longer allow our past to determine our shame and disabilities to continue to be hidden under a mask.

Unmasking, will show those around us, that we are no longer holding on to our insecurities of fear. We will be comfortable with ourselves and have no need to try to please others. Many of us go through life hiding behind masks, but God calls His followers to honesty. Honesty brings about transformation. And transformation ultimately results in peace. Unmasking can free us from the pain of pretense and lead us to the blessing of deeper fellowship with God's people. God wants us to be able to feel free and to be free, for the purposed He has called us. We are not to be labeled by other and be made to be someone that we are not. we are worthy to Jesus, because He made us worthy in Him. We must begin to allow the liberty He has given to us to be who He purposed us to be for Himself.

Stop allowing those around you to dictate who you are and begin to love the person that God designed you to be for himself. Be proud of the design that your creator has made. So, get rid of the mask, and be the real you.

Chapter 3

Embracing the Real You

How can we embrace our Image? How will we be able to embrace this image that we see in the mirror? How can we see ourselves the way God sees us.? All we see is hurt and pain from our experience of childhood, and adulthood. All we see is the bad things that we have done to ourselves and others.

Our God doesn't want us to focus on those things but focus on Him and know that you are fearfully and wonderfully made by Him. He wants you to begin loving Him and embracing His love for you. It is not where you are now, that defines His love. He loves you no matter what you have done. He is the God that cares about His creation and wants us to embrace His design.

Let's answer some of these questions about embrace. What is an embrace? It is to take or receive gladly or eagerly; accept willingly.

The first question will be to embrace God, when you embrace God, then you will be able to embrace you. When you realize the truth about who you are in Him, then you will no longer look for substitutes to replace your image. You will not continue to look at your shame, but to look at the grace that God has given unto you to be complete in Him.

The second question is to allow God Word to govern your life. Believe what God has spoken concerning you. Hold on to more of His Word than your own or others. Know that you are special to God, because He made you in His Image and in His likeness. Embrace His word in your life, believe in it and apply it to your life. When you begin to embrace who you are in Him, then you will be able to see yourself as He does. Guess What! You are beautiful to Him.

Just remember that you didn't evolve but was created and designed with a purpose.

And the blueprints of our lives may be similar to others, but we are uniquely designed.

The Lord wants us to know, He designed our look, so that it pleases Him, He created us not to do our own thing, but to appreciate His Handiwork. He desires a personal relationship with His Beloved.

Your soul has a hole in it that needs to be filled with Your Creator. We will never find fulfillment in life without Him filling us with His presence. We will continue to look for other things and chase after other things to embrace ourselves. Our God loves us so much and He wants the same love in return. We were designed with an intense need of our Creator, God.

Without a relationship with Him, we will always be searching for something to fill that void. Examples of our chase: Drugs, food, Alcohol, material things, sex, occupations, and other things.

They are all temporary fixes, that can easily be discarded, and we are still left empty. Jesus is the only one that can fill the void that we may be feeling. He is the only one that can give us our worth. We must believe that we are beautiful to Him. In all reality, He is the only one that matters. We must take note of this, when we finally understand who God is, it will help us to find peace about ourselves in Him. When we begin to lean on Him and trust Him then we will change. The clay can't tell the potter how to design His own masterpiece, we must know we are made by design. We as believer's wanting to tell the creator how to shape us and mold us.

God has the right to mold and shape us however He pleases. We must take note that we are here on this earth for His purposes. He has designed each one of us to do His will. So, when we continue to look at ourselves, and marvel over our beauty from a variety of substances, we tell our creator, "I really don't like the way you made me" so," I am going to correct what I don't like about myself."

Have you ever thought of how God feels when we change all our imperfections, whatever they may be? Have we come to be able to accept the image that God has given to us for His purpose of our existence?

This book is not to judge those who feel the need to wear makeup, or have other enhancements done; It just to let you know that you are beautiful just the way God has made you. You do not need to seek after the world's beauty, but seek God for the beauty within. Our Heavenly Father made us the way He wanted us to be for Himself.

He knew when He created us, all the features that He wanted us to have. Remember, we are His handiwork. We as believer's say "I must put these lashes on and do my weave, so I can look good for my King". Which King are you preferring? Because if we are talking about Jesus, those things are not important to Him. Truly it is the beauty from within. Our sole purpose is to love the Lord our God, with all our mind, soul, and strength. We should not continue to run or crave after vanity; we must be willing to be molded and shaped by the word of God to accomplish His will in the earth.

We have heard the saying, "My face is beat to the gods' 'What god are you preferring? It is certainly not Jesus. We need to get out of this careless way of thinking. What turns Jesus head towards us is our inner beauty. We even call ourselves Diva for Christ, are you Serious? Do you know what Diva means? Let talk about some of its definition

(a) a female deity the basic sense of the term is goddess. (b) in Italian the term is used to celebrate an extremely talented opera singer.

Now, a goddess is a deity to be worshiped. In the word of God, we are not to worship no other God but Him. We must not present ourselves as an Idol to distract others away from God. Now, if we look at the urban dictionary, the word diva is a female hustler, a woman who must have her way, and may be a bit rude, who belittles people, and believes that everyone is beneath her, she is selfish, spoiled and overly dramatic. (veracitywoman.wordpress.com)

Allowing Him to mold each one of us for soul winning. That's important to Him. I know some of us may not agree with these statements that are being made. Yes, everyone has their own opinion concerning modern day fashion and looks. We truly want to turn the heads of people, through compliments. However, we need to turn our King's head by the way we live our lives. Are we beautifying the flesh, and leaving our soul a mess?

When it comes to our King, it is all about our soul surrendering to the Kingdom of God. The Lord wants you to embrace your inner beauty and what He has created you to look like for Him, We are not to be affirmed by makeup, breast enhancements, eye lashes, different color eyes, or the latest fashion, but we are to affirmed by His love for us as His Bride. We must embrace who we are as His workmanship, in what He is developing us to be for His divine purpose. The Lord has so much in store for us as He is restoring what has been marred and corrupted by the tongues of men.

He is fulfilling His purpose for our very lives. He is showing us through His word how He is making us whole in Him. He is taking out what we do not need and helping us discover who we really are in Him. Our beauty is to reflect who He is to those who do not know Him. Our beauty is to demonstrate the love He has for us and others. We are not subject to the opinions of men, but to what the Lord God has spoken concerning us. So, embrace who the Lord our creator has designed us to become for Him. We shouldn't allow the conformity of this world to swallow us up with its vanity.

Discover our true beauty in the Lord. Give Him the opportunity to change the very essence of who we are. When we have the right attitude to embrace ourselves, then we are able to be pleased with His design. When we are able to embrace who we are in Christ, it gives us the full knowledge of our purpose for the Kingdom of God, He gives you a sense of completeness. Our king has designed us for purpose. It's time to get the enemy of our soul out of our heads, and out of the mirror that we are using.

It is time to embrace the true us. The real us are lying dormant inside of our being. The real embrace is that we will allow Jesus to continue the work on the inside of us. Only, Jesus can deliver us from the lies that have been plaguing us all our life. When we allow Jesus to deliver us, then we will not focus on the outer us and begin to embrace the inner us.

Isaiah tell us like this:

[Isa 45:9-10 KJV] 9 Woe unto him that striveth with his Maker! [Let] the potsherd [strive] with the potsherds of the earth. Shall the clay say to him that fashioneth it, What makest thou? or thy work, He hath no hands? 10 Woe unto him that saith unto [his] father, what begettest thou? or to the woman, what hast thou brought forth?

This is what Isaiah is saying, Our God, as creator, know what He is making. He is the one who has purposed us to be whatever, He has designed for us to be. In essence, who are we to complain about what the potter has made?

[Rom 9:21 KJV] 21 Hath not the potter power over the clay, of the same lump to make one vessel unto honour, and another unto dishonour?

For our King it is all about our soul surrendering to Him for the Kingdom of God. The Lord wants you to embrace your inner beauty and what He has created you to look like for Him,

We are not affirmed by makeup, breast enhancements, eye lashes, different color eyes, or the latest fashion, but we are affirmed by

His love for us as His Bride. We must embrace who we are as His workmanship, in what He is developing us to be for His divine purpose. The Lord has so much in store for us as he is restoring what has been marred and corrupted by the tongues of men.

When you are able to embrace who you are in Christ, it gives you the full knowledge of your purpose for the Kingdom of God, He gives you a sense of completeness, to know you are following and embracing Jesus' way of thinking by the transformation of your mind. It's not hard to see yourself the way that your king has designed you. Get the enemy of your soul out of your head, and out of the mirror that you are using to look at yourself. It is time to embrace the true you. The real you are lying dormant inside of your being. The real embrace is that you will allow Jesus to continue the work on the inside of you

Only, Jesus can deliver you from the lies that have been plaguing you all your life. When you allow Jesus to deliver you, then you will not focus on the outer you and begin to embrace the inner you.

Matthew 22:37 KJV

37 Jesus said unto him, thou shalt love the Lord thy God with all thy heart, and with all thy soul, and with all thy mind.

38 This is the first and great commandment.

The question is how can you love you without loving God? I am not talking about the world's way of loving you, but the creator's way of loving yourself. It takes you to learn how to really love your God, and to appreciate who you are in Him. It's not about all the things we do to enhance our flesh man, but it is all that we do to appreciate him, and how He perfectly made us for His Glory. We all have a unique look about ourselves, that proves that we are fearfully and wonderfully made.

We lost our uniqueness, when we were told that we were not beautiful enough, or a boyfriend or a husband, told us that we didn't have what it takes to be with them. So, some of us eat our way through our hurts and pains and we find ourselves into a deep depression, and not caring about the way we look, and some of us have brought everything and we spent all our money trying to look the part, to make everyone else accept us. When we are killing our soul, with the world's mess of values. We are destroying ourselves with what will look good and not focusing on who makes me look good.

Chapter 4

Loving God

With our Lord and Savior, it is truly all about souls. Your soul being cleanse by His blood and knowing your identity in Him. (Jesus) without knowing who you are, will crippled us, in believing that we are to look a certain way to please our King. Our king loves us the way we are, if we have scars, it's to identify ourselves in Him. Remembering that He was scared for us.

Loving God is the first step in loving ourselves.

Spending time in His presence, soaks away all the ugliness, we may see in ourselves, when we look into the mirror. When we soak in His presence it helps us to forget about us and how we feel or look at ourselves. We must rid ourselves from what others think. We as His Bride need to get away from thinking in that manner. On this journey we are on, and whatever we had to endure was to help someone else on their journey, it's to tell others how your King helped us to overcome the obstacles that came up against us. Some of us will argue about it doesn't matter how we look if our heart is right towards

God, and He doesn't care if we wear our worldly enhancements if we feel good about ourselves.

Sorry, to say, He does care, He wants our focus to be about Him and doing the Will of the Father, He wants to build up our self-esteem, and to build and shape our character for His kingdom. The Lord wants others to see our inner beauty and show who He is to this dying world. We live in a world that states it's all about me, myself and I, can we be honest as a believer it's all about Jesus.

Our Bible is a book that we hold so dear, it's His Words that make a difference in a dying society. Loving God deserves our true focus, let examine what Jesus was saying in Matthew 22:37

Let's look at the word heart which in Strong's concordance **Heart** is *kardia,* which denotes the central of all physical and spiritual life. The soul or mind, as it is the fountain and seat of the thoughts, passions, purposes, endeavors, of the understanding, the faculty and seat of the intelligence.

Soul is the *psyche*, which means breath, the breath of life, the vital force which animates the body and shows itself in breathing. In the human soul in so far as it is constituted that by the right use of the aids offered it by God it can attain its highest end and secure eternal blessedness, the soul regarded as a moral being designed for everlasting life.

Mind in the Strong concordance, *dianoia,* means the mind as a faculty of understanding, feeling, desiring.

As we can see that it takes every part of who we are to love God the way that we should. God should be our everything, meaning, it goes beyond the very fabric of our beings. We say that we love Him, however, we fall short of showing Him how much we love him. Jesus tells us in Matthew 15:8 *These people draweth nigh unto me with their mouth, and honoureth me with their lips; but their heart is far from me.*

This is Jesus talking! He also told us that if we love Him, we will keep His commandments. (John 14:15 KJV) We must remember that keeping God's command is His will that is in His word and his commandments is in our hearts, and for the most part, these commandments have to do with our inner life, not our outward life. We live in a world where everything goes, and we walk around in the body of Christ with no accountability. We get upset when we make choices based on our temporal feelings. When we are questioned about why we are doing different things to our body; The first thing we have to say is "it's my body and I will do what pleases me." Now, did we forget that when it comes to Christ our body now belongs to Him. Did we not know that we gave up ownership back to the one who created us? I think we did forget that we were bought with a price. (*1Corinthians 6:19-20 19 What? Know ye not that your body is the temple of the Holy Ghost, which is in you, which ye have of God, and ye are not your own. 20. for ye were bought at a price; therefore, glorify God in your body and in your spirit, which are God's)*

Please understand that the love of God is truly in what He has created for Himself. We are in this earth realm to please the Father. We are so accustomed to doing what pleases us and not truly thinking about what pleases God. Let's allow our Lord, Our King to be what matters most in this temporal realm we are in. Let us truly evaluate who and what we mean to Him, and not ourselves. It is very easy to compete and covet the look of another, we must love God our heavenly and be focused on what pleases Him. God shapes our very being into who He is!

We all need to take notes from His word that He proposes to us for His good pleasure. Philippians 2:13 for it is God which worketh in you both to will and to do of His good pleasure. Our development is to secure and purpose in Him. We are to do His good pleasure.

Loving God is the very essence of who we are. God is love, which means that His unconditional love for us is deeper than what we can image. Every part of us, has within us, the love for our Creator, that was put in us. We must discover it, by spending ample amount of time in His presence.

Spending time in His presence, transform your very existence.

It will allow your focus to be all about what pleases Him. It will give you the gratification that you need. It will give you the peace to rest in Him. Your love for Him will take your mind off of your appearances and how you feel about yourself.

Here are a few ways that we can show God that we love Him:
1) Obey His Word John 14:15 KJV
2) Worship Him in the beauty of Holiness Psalm 29:4 KJV
3) Pray to Him without ceasing 1Thessalonians 5:16-18 KJV
4) Love others as yourself Matthew 33:37 KJV
5) Reverence the Lord Hebrews 12:28 KJV

Show the Lord how much you love him by cultivating your relationship with Him. Allow Him to be first in your life for real. Spend that time with Him that He desires for you. When we allow Him to take precedence in our life, we will be the better person. It will allow us to be intwine in Him. We will show Him that He is all that we need in this world and in the world to come. We will be so into Him, that it will not matter what those around of us thinks of our outer image. Our focus will be on him and the His perfect will for our lives.

Loving God is the ultimate way to learn how to love ourselves and others. When we realize who we are in God, then we will be able to embrace Him and others. Also, we will be more selfless, than selfish. We will see ourselves in the eyes of our Creator and see others the way He sees them.

Loving God gives us the divine opportunity to feel His love for us. We are His own possession and He claims us His own. We are His delight and the apple of His eyes. The Father love for us is unconditional and everlasting love that draws us closer to Him. In Songs of Solomon, in chapter 7:10 (NIV) *"the Lord your God is with you, the mighty Warrior who saves. He will take great delight in you' In his love will no longer rebuke you, but will rejoice over you with singing."*

The lord bought me to the banqueting house, and His banner over me was love. Song of Solomon 2:4 this let us know how the Lord proclaims His love for His bride. We are His bride, whom He simply adores. He is not a shame of us, he wants us to love Him back, with the love that He shows toward us. He wants us to know this great love that is indescribable. Our finite mind is unable to conceive that type of love.

His banner over us is to acknowledge us publicly that He is our spouse and we are His Bride. Isn't that Great! It doesn't matter what we look like to Him, He is our Creator that is designing each stages of our lives. Each stage of life, will give only Him the Glory for His design. The Lord is pleading with us to come back to His Heart and give Him our all. Loving our God is His desire from us. He wants us to think about Him first before anything else. Intimacy is the key that will bring true relationship with Him. So, love Him with your who heart and love Him with all your soul, and last but not least, love Him with all your mind.

When you begin this process, then the cares of this world will not matter to us. It will be only Him. we will see our beauty from His eyes, not ours. In this process, it will give us the divine opportunity to be designed and purpose for His good pleasure. It will help us to be fully develop to do what He has called each of us to do for Him. Let's show our God how much we appreciate and value Him over this world system. Let us find our true value in His love for us. As we offer up our love for Him, it will satisfy our hungry souls from developing unhealthy desires that are not worth anything.

Chapter 5

Loving Yourself

Now let's talk about loving ourselves. Our bible offers us basic instructions on how we can live healthy, spiritual lives, while here on earth. We must embrace Jesus Christ and His sacrifice and be at peace concerning our lives. Being a healthy and spiritual human being is knowing who God is and how we can learn from Him to be who He has called us to be. Sometimes because of some life issues and pressures, we may not know how to love ourselves. What do I mean? I mean we have allowed others to dictate who we are and what we should look like.

We look in a mirror and get a reflection on our looks, then we say "I don't like this, and I don't like that". "God, why have you made me this way?" "I am ugly and I don't like myself or love what you have made." So, "I will reverse what my creator has made by changing all of what I think is wrong".

We are driven to do all sorts of things to belong and to feel good about ourselves. All we need is a dose of Jesus and begin to love Him in the way we should and then we will be able to appreciate His handiwork and love ourselves.

Can I be honest here, I had a problem with my image, that I wanted to change my looks, by dying my hair, colored contacts, and make up. I found all those enhancements empty. They held no real value. People used to say, "you are vain" I used to say, no I am not, it doesn't matter if I change the way I look!" I am doing it for my king. We must love ourselves beyond the measures of what man thinks, including ourselves.

Jesus makes it very clear in the Bible that it's essential to love God and love others. These are the two greatest commandments and examples of great love that we are all called to have. It ensures us that we can love ourselves and others

When we love ourselves, it is finding out about our God. Our identity should not be based on our whims but be fully based on God's love for us and appreciate His way of creating us for his purposes.

Loving ourselves, will allow us to love others as ourselves, it will help us to get from the place of vain, to the place of true love for ourselves. We must be aware of the world's way of conformity. We must know that our Lord and Savior wants us to be able to live a life pleasing to himself. True happiness comes from knowing Jesus and loving Him.

Self-Love is about recognizing God's plan for our lives. When things feel out of control or we feel lost, turn to God and ask for guidance that speaks of His undying love for us.

The Bible does speak to us about being lovers of ourselves. While we should love ourselves by ensuring we have spiritual, physical and emotional health. We should not be self-obsessed about ourselves in a way that is displeasing to God. 2Timothy talked about the end times, and we are a pure image of loving ourselves more than we ought. We will put people down and speak in a negative way if they don't fit into our mold of how they should look. These people around us must resemble us. They must have the latest fashions, hair weave, makeup and other enhancements to belong to your group. Do you really think that Our King Jesus is pleased with that? We can look at the different accounts of the four gospels and determine what was important to Him. It was not our outer look. His mission was to show us how to live for the Kingdom of God.

This book was not written to condemn anyone, it's what the Holy Spirit led for this hour that we are in. Our journey is with the Lord. This information is to address what the real beauty of God's Kingdom looks like. We are in the last hour when our soon coming king will arrive to get those who belong to Him. Are you a part of this world or do you belong to Him? Outward appearances are not what makes us great for the kingdom of God, it's what the Holy Spirit does on the inside of us to bring out our true love for Him and others, and identify us in His kingdom.

We are to love ourselves, in the light of how our creator loves us. When we love Him and love ourselves unselfishly, then we can love ourselves in the right light of God's Love. Everyone must someday meet our Lord and Savior; please don't let your works of keeping up with the world be your downfall and missing your place in the kingdom. If we are not conformed and we are transformed, then we will be able to prove what is good, and acceptable to our God.

Romans 12:2

And be not conformed to this world; but be ye transformed by the renewing of your mind, that ye may prove what is that good, and acceptable, and perfect will of God.

KJV

Proverb 198 KJV *He that getteth wisdom loveth his own soul: he that keepeth understanding shall find good.*

We are to love ourselves toward the importance of our souls. This proverb verse encourages us to love our own soul so much that we find goodness and truth, this goodness and truth is freely found in Jesus Christ. Our spiritual health and beauty are forming an intimate relationship with Christ. It is Jesus who can fulfill the beauty within us. He wants us to show the World our inner beauty more than the outward beauty that we so desire.

We are not be so content with our interests, but also the needs of others. Why is it so hard to care for the needs of others? Could it be that we are so consumed with us, that we lose interest in others? We are supposed to be the church of the Lord Jesus Christ, yet still we are all about our self-image to the point of spending all we have to look good on the outside.

Loving ourselves is when we allow the Master of our soul to design us as He chooses. We are to be complete and whole within Him. When we look for all other things to fill the void in our lives, it leaves us empty. When we show our love to others from the effect and impact that Jesus gives us; then we can feel good about ourselves.

When we understand the Love of God, then we can love ourselves and others. We will be able to embrace our natural look without any enhancements and feel good about it. We will not be so consumed about who will give us compliments on what we look like or what we have on our body. We will be satisfied with the love of God and a godly love for ourselves, that will give us a genuine love for others that are on our path.

Now, we don't want to continue in the ungodly love of ourselves, that causes us to be arrogant and conceited. 2 Timothy 3:1-2 KJV tells us *"this know also, that in the last days perilous times shall come. For men shall be lovers of their own selves, covetous, boasters, proud, blasphemers, disobedient to parents, unthankful, unholy."*

Proverbs 16:3 KJV *"commit thy works unto the Lord, and thy thoughts shall be established"*

When we align ourselves with the Lord, our total perspective of the way we look will change. We can better love ourselves when we know what it is God wants of us. This life that we have been given by our heavenly father is to know Him through His word. We need to embrace ourselves and love ourselves just the way He loves us. How can we do that? It is when we let go of our selfishness and become selfless and follow the Holy Spirit.

Proverbs 23:7 KJV "*7 For as he thinketh in his heart, so is he:*" *Eat and drink, saith he to thee; but his heart is not with thee.*

Now, this verse here is letting us know that it's whatever, we think about ourselves that allows us to remain in that way. If we say that we are ugly, then we are going to feel that way, why? Because we spoke it into the atmosphere, and we made a confession on what we think, instead of speaking God's word concerning us.

Here are 10 steps to loving yourself:
1) Start telling yourself what you love about yourself. Be kind to yourself with the Word of God.
2) Be one with yourself by seeing yourself beautiful, the way God made you.
3) Focus less on winning the approval of others, and don't let others define who you are.
4) Distance yourself from those who bring you down. Love yourself enough to be in good relationships, rather than bad ones.
5) Forgive your past self when you confront the dark parts of yourself, allow Jesus to deliver you and repent for not approving of your very existence. Ask Jesus to help you forgive those who abuse and took advantage of you for selfish reasoning.
6) Start making the change you know you need to make by seeing the changes in your life that must take place. You will have to do things that you have never done before.
7) Believe in your abilities and identify who you are in Christ and begin the process of transformation in Jesus Christ.
8) See the beauty from within, and the wholeness of your beauty in Jesus Christ
9) See yourself set free and deliver in Jesus Name.
10) Be cultivated in the nine fruit of the spirit of God. (MarcandAngel.com)

Chapter 6

Giving your Heart Back to God

We think that we have given our total heart to God, which we did not! Our hearts bend on what we want and what we desire. We talk about a good game, but if the truth be told; it's all about us. Our heavenly Father wants us to get out of our love for the world and put our heart back on Him. We have truly missed the mark about our true love for God. Our love for Him has been all about lip service, and our heart is far from Him. (Matthew 15:8 KJV)

When we truly give our hearts to God, we will stop worrying about all that we can't control. We begin to trust, we let the little things roll off our back. We know that our heart is in a safe place, and we find comfort knowing our God will never leave us. We must realize that we have been putting our trust into the wrong things or people, and instead of trying so desperately to understand the world, or confused, wondering which direction to take, we can find calm and peace. We must know that we are protected and loved, unconditionally, by our Savior.

Giving our hearts to God empowers us, to do His will for our lives. His promises are to protect us and strengthen us for His word and for each day. When we stop relying on ourselves or other imperfect people to guide our heart and decisions, then are we able to realize He has been paving our path all the time, and when we trust Him to take control, to love and direct us, we will find strength that only He(Jesus) can give.

Sometimes we get so wrapped up in this world that we get entangled into romantic relationships. We fall into habits and patterns with other people. We begin to see our things and possessions as a measure of our worth. But God sees otherwise. He knows what the material things of this world mean nothing a matter of fact it leads us empty. He knows that our true value rests in Him. He longs for us to see the worth of our souls rather than our temporary bodies.

When we give our heart to God, we will begin to value our relationship and will be able to build upon His love. We can start to see the value in our personality, what's in our hearts and be able to impact those who are connected to us. Food for thought! It will not matter in the next life how much money you have, nor your status here in the earth realm.

Giving our heart back to God is finding our true value in this life. Giving your heart to God will help us to be all that He has purposed us to be for his Kingdom. When we give our hearts totally to Him, we will find a new purpose and a new sense of self.

When we give our heart to God, we will stop worrying about all those things we are unable to control. We will begin to trust the Lord and turn our hearts back to Him. we will leave the comforts of what we desire and lean and focus on what He desires. Peace is waiting on the sidelines, when we decide to pick it up and find our true comfort in God. Giving our hearts back to God will strengthen us through life's pressures. It will enable us to completely trust Him for all our life needs.

As soon as the opportunity makes itself known, it will give us a chance to know that we need God for everything. It's very hard to consider life without Him. Without Him, we are unable to do anything that would be beneficial to anyone. When we allow Him to take back control of our lives, then we will find the strength, we can achieve through Him.

Guess What? We will begin to put value into the right places and people. It will help us not to be so concerned with how we may look and appeal to others. We will be satisfied in the way we look and be in the right mindset to compliment someone else's instead of waiting for a compliment. Our focus will be on the things of God rather than our interest in the things of this world. All our affection will be what matters to God. What are His desires and how we may be able to please Him?

We get so wrapped up in this world, that we truly lose focus on what really matters. We fall into different habits that steal our time from the Lord.

Matthew 6:21 KJV *"For where your treasure is, there your heart will be also."*

Our God knows that the material things of this world means nothing. His main interest is the true value of where we will rest when we leave this life. And he longs for us to see the worth of our souls rather than our temporary bodies.

Don't be fooled by the set up in this world. We have a strong spirit of vanity that has swept the nation. Our interest and investments are all about our temporal appearance. We are fooling ourselves to think that the way we look for the world is the way that pleases our King. What truly pleases Him is us loving Him, spending time with Him, and investing our time in the things of His Kingdom.

When we give our hearts back to God it will help us to value relationships that build and not tear down, we will start to see the value in our personality, in our impact on others.

Joel 2:13 KJV

13 Rend your hearts and not your garments and return to the Lord, your God, for He is gracious and merciful, slow to anger, and abounding in loving-kindness; and He revokes His sentence of evil [when His conditions are met].

Our Heavenly Father is more concerned with the condition of our hearts, not how we look or what we wear. It's vital for us to be able to position our hearts back to the Father. It's time to truly turn our backs on Babylon, and its corruption of sin, and turn back to God with our whole hearts. This life that we live is not for us, but for our Heavenly Father.

It's time for us to obey His commands and do the Will of the Father. It's truly not a talent show, or a Miss America pageant, but genuinely giving the Father, our hearts. What this passage is saying to each of us, is it's not your fashions, or your makeup, but it is about turning your heart to your King. what makes the Father smile is when His children obey His Word, and value what He has placed before them. The second part to this verse is He is always graciously waiting for us to leave this world behind and conform to His way of doing things.

Zechariah 1:3 KJV

3 *Therefore say to them [the Jews of this day], Thus says the Lord of hosts: Return to Me, says the Lord of hosts, and I will return to you; it is the utterance of the Lord of hosts.*

God is warning us, and speaking to us, about this present world we live in. He wants us to turn our back on the evilness of this world. He wants us to be sold out for Him and pay attention to His leading. The Lord is saying here return to Me and I will return to you. There is so much in ministry that the Lord has charged us His leading ladies to do. It truly is more than worrying about a Gucci Bag, or Dolce and Gabbana bag or shoes. Those things are nice, but not important. You are making these fashion designers rich, while you are in poverty for lack of managing your affairs. Some of you may say, "Well, sister, I don't know what you're talking about, I love God and my Designer's things too. As, long as I pay my bills and look good, there's nothing you can say. The Holy Spirit is saying how much are you giving to others for the Kingdom? Are you helping the poor in their time of need? Are you managing your money that will please God? How Much are you giving to the poor? How much are you taking care of the orphans, or widows?

It's all about us being a blessing to others, Loving God and others. Showing your light of Jesus to others.

Think about it! How beneficial would it be to be all made up and deck out in your designer wear, and a bum on the street has dirty clothes and no food to eat? It would not be beneficial; Why? Because that bum on the street may be homeless without food to eat. We are the only Jesus that some people will ever see. Are we in tune with the Holy Spirit that we can discern a need?

All I am saying, we need to get back to the Gospel of the Lord Jesus Christ. We need to feed the hungry, give shelter to those who may be in need. We need to learn not to heap our material things on ourselves. Jesus shared.

Nehemiah 1:9 KJV

9 But if you return to Me and keep My commandments and do them, though your outcasts were in the farthest part of the heavens [the expanse of outer space], yet will I gather them from there and will bring them to the place in which I have chosen to set My [a]Name.

This verse is saying once again, turn away from yourselves, and the world and turn back to Him. Keep His Word and your loved one's will be gathered to the place where the Lord has chosen to set His name. It's all about doing what God has commanded. Heed His Word, do His Word, and all that has been promised, will be manifested. Stop looking at you in the world sense.

The lord is saying "My wayward and wandering children, turn back! Turn to Me! The path you're on is one that leads to destruction. One I can't bless. But it's not too late! You haven't wandered too far. You can stop right now, right where you are and return your heart back to Me. You can make a wise decision and choose Me. Repent of your sins and receive the fullness of My mercy; I welcome every part of you to come to Me so I can fix you. You can't fix yourself; it will take the Holy Spirit of God to fix all the unwanted things that lie deep within the heart.

The Lord is pleading! Don't delay! Come to today! My salvation is free! Let (Me) Jesus make you beautiful, Let Me purify your soul. Let Me crown you with the beauty for ashes, the oil of Joy instead of mourning, and a garment of praise instead of a spirit of despair. The Lord is saying, you worry about your outer man, I am concerned about the inner man that I will be called it oaks of righteousness, a planting of the Lord for the display of His splendor. (Isaiah 61:3

Our God desire for us to return to Him with our whole heart, He long for us His bride to stop chasing after our spiritual lovers, and turn back to Him. Lord is saying, why I am not enough for you? Why can't you trust Me to make you beautiful? Did you not know you are so beautiful? It doesn't matter all the things that you have done to turn your heart away. The spirit of vanity has swayed you away from Me. It has been all about the culture attractions that has captivate your hearts. Come out of vanity my precious daughter. Just like in the love story found in Hosea. I demonstrated by love for Israel, through Hosea. The Father was ready to accept His bride, even though she was found in a shameful state. The Father love for us, allow His only begotten son, Jesus to come and died for our sins, and return us back to our true love. His precious blood return us back to the Father's Heart. He wants his daughters to find joy in Him, and delight in His love. When we as the Father's daughter, realize the true unconditional love from Him, then we will be able turn our hearts back to him.

Looking at Hosea 2:6 KJV "Therefore, behold, I will hedge up thy way with thorn, and make a wall, that she shall not find her paths. 7 and she shall follow after her lovers, but she shall not overtake them; and she shall seek them, but shall not find them; then shall she say, I will go and return to my first husband; for then was it better with me than now.

Let think about this, we are in the now, in our chase for worldly things, when those things begin to change on us, then we look around and find our selves empty. Our face wrinkle up and droopy and our body looking not attractive, because we have worn our body out with the extra things that we have found appealing.

We look at this scripture and say, this message in Hosea is about, being a prostitute in cheating on a husband. If we are not unaware, we have prostitute ourselves to vanity. We have been driven by that spirit, that it totally consumes our time. It has put us in a prison, and told us that we will not be beautiful without her. She dictates how we feel, what we look like, all through her mirror.

If there were never a mirror or reflection of ourselves, we would not be so consumed by the way we look. Wow! Think about that! Was it ever a thought that we are unable to see our spirit and soul? It hidden all in our fleshy appearance. Yet, we don't put much focus on it. We say, as long as I look good on the outside, my insides will be just fine.

My material things keep me going, and when I get to the end of this road, I will tell God, now here I am ready to return to you. Your Spirit and soul matters to God. It's where your discovery of true beauty lives. Will it be too late? Will we have enough time to repent and turn to Him. Daughters of Zion, come out of your adulteress ways and give yourself to your husband Jesus Christ. Allow Him to make you beautiful. Truly that's Jesus Heart toward His Bride, He is saying turn your heart back! I desire you my beloved. Jesus is at the door of your hearts, saying come unto Me" My precious daughters get out of this world system, it is weighing you down, with its expectations. Begin to focus on your purpose that I have for you. Focus on your eternal estate in heaven with Me." He is saying to us, He is all we need in this earth.

Mark 8:36 KJV *What profit a man, if she shall gain the whole world, and lose his own soul?* Wow! Sisters, do you see that! We must turn back to our first love; we must begin to appreciate Him for all

He has done for us. We must bow our knees to Him and not this world and all that it has to offer.

Jesus was speaking through the prophet Hosea, *"My people are destroyed for lack of knowledge; because thou hast rejected knowledge, I will also reject thee, that thou shalt be no priest to me; seeing thou hast forgotten the law of thy God, I will also forget thy children.* What is being said here? You will go to the world for your knowledge instead of seeking His face for the knowledge. We have strayed away from His Word and walking around in a mist of confusion. The word priest is a person whose office is to perform or make sacrificial offerings. *1 Peter 2:9 tells us that we are a royal priesthood, a holy nation, a peculiar people; that ye should shew forth the praises of him who hath called you out of darkness into his marvelous light;*

Chapter 7

Turning away from the Spirit of Vanity

Turning away from the spirit of Vanity is not as hard as you may think. It's a matter of realizing that it's more to this life that meets the eye. If we were not so consumed in the mirror, we will be able to walk away from the vanity of this world. Did you not know that you would not be able to take your makeup, your fashion nor your designer's shoes to the next transition of life. Yes, there is life after this one. Where will you spend eternity? Some of us may say, well, I know that I am going to heaven. I am a church goer, and I do my devotions, and I pay my tithes, and offering and I sow my seeds to my leader. Okay! The real question is do you have a personal relationship with Jesus? Are you under the leading of The Holy Spirit or an unholy spirit?

What does **Vanity** mean? It means excessive pride in one's appearance, qualities, abilities, achievements, etc., also a lack of real value, hollowness, worthlessness, the vanity of a selfish life.

Let's take a closer look at the cosmetics industry that makes billions of dollars annually, there are women of all age groups that wear makeup to enhance their natural look. Here's a question: is painting your face "fashionable to God?

We have a conception that it is pleasing to God, why wouldn't He want me to look good for Him? Let look at the world of God concerning this vanity.

Psalm 39:5-6 KJV *"verily truly every man at his best state is altogether Vanity … surely every man walks in a vain show an image "Vanity is a powerful force that drives a human being.* Our modern-day society strives on looking good and being beautiful. Here's a little statistic of the plastic surgery reports that over 18 million people had cosmetic procedures in the United States in 2018. Cosmetic surgery aims to improve your appearance.

Let take a look at some ancient Roots:

The origin of makeup is evidence from the Egyptian tombs dating to 3500BC

"By the first century AD the Egyptian, Roman, Greek and Middle Eastern cultures had developed cosmetics to whiten skin by powers, and to darken eyelids, eyelashes, and eyebrows, they used kohl. For their cheeks, they used rouge. (presenttruthmn.com)

As we can see that naturally cosmetic formed from Egypt but before Egypt, Semiramis is known as the mother of all harlots. He used makeup as well as suggestive provocative clothing for various religious and sexual rituals.

The first women to wear makeup were prostitutes! They were those who changed their appearances by facial paint, which was a custom. (rcg.com)

Jeremiah 4:30 KJV

Now that the history of cosmetics has been established, the deeper subject is what the Bible has to say about it for us to say, "I never saw that in the Bible," or" that was under the law." God Word is His Word from Genesis to Revelation. We as a people have continuously separated the Old Testament from the New testament.

We must remember that the Bible contents are parallel to each other. Old or New.

The actual words makeup, cosmetics, lipstick, mascara, etc. are not found in the Bible, but direct references to makeup and eye paint are found in three places, possibly four. *Jeremiah 4:30 KJV describes how modern Israel has fallen into the conduct of a whore among the nations. "Though you deck yourself with ornaments of gold though you rented your face with painting, in vain shall you make yourself fair (beautiful) your lovers will despise you, they will seek your life"*

Just like Ancient Israel, who always sought to be like those nations around her. Israel was supposed to be an example. We are supposed to be an example to those around us, but we as a nation want to belong and fit in to this world system We quote often, I will not be conformed to this world, but I will be transformed by the renewing of my mind, to do what is good, acceptable and the perfect will of God. Do we really know God's perfect will? Some of us will use the Old Testament to make certain points, but when it comes to correction, we say "we are not under the Law". Women of today think they just want to "look nice" to the world, when they really look like prostitutes to God." (rcg.org)

I recommend you read the entire article in the above website. It's time to stop picking out what we like in the Bible, and accept the entire Bible

[Eze 23:40 KJV] 40 And furthermore, that ye have sent for men to come from far, unto whom a messenger [was] sent; and, lo, they came: for whom thou didst wash thyself, painted thy eyes, and decked thyself with ornaments,

Ezekiel parallels Jeremiah, letting us know that God reinforces what He said. Women of the modern world please take note and this warning Please be careful that you do not conclude that you are an exception to the punishment foretold in this prophecy. God connects eye paint directly to seduction for valorous purposes.

It's time to seek God on what He desires more than your own

opinion or My opinion. Truly I was one that wore makeup, but the Lord took me through the scriptures and the Holy Spirit of God convicted me. Now, this subject is totally between you and the Lord. The Holy Spirit led me to write about this controversial topic. I know you properly mentioned what about Queen Esther. It does not say she painted her face; it does state six months with oil or myrrh ad six months with spices and ointments for women. (Esther 2:12 KJV)

We are called to be the Bride of Christ and We are beautiful, just the way He has made us. We are to please Him, not ourselves. "Well, some will say my husband likes my long hair, and my makeup and my designer wear, so to please him my husband, I am going to continue to wear all of the above things mentioned. I have to keep myself up for my man." What about Jesus your Husband? Are you willing to please Him? Do you have the focus of pleasing Him? Let not be like the foolish virgins (Matthew 25:2-13 KJV) *Then the kingdom of heaven shall be likened to ten virgins who took their lamps and went to meet the bridegroom.* **2** *Five of them were foolish (thoughtless, without forethought) and five were wise (sensible, intelligent, and prudent).*

3 *For when the foolish took their lamps, they did not take any [extra] oil with them;* **4** *But the wise took flasks of oil along with them [also] with their lamps.* **5** *While the bridegroom lingered and was slow in coming, they all began nodding their heads, and they fell asleep.* **6** *But at midnight there was a shout, Behold, the bridegroom! Go out to meet him!* **7** *Then all those virgins got up and put their own lamps in order.* **8** *And the foolish said to the wise, give us some of your oil, for our lamps are going out.* **9** *But the wise replied, There will not be enough for us and for you; go instead to the dealers and buy for yourselves.* **10** *But while they were going away to buy, the bridegroom came, and those who were prepared went in with him to the marriage feast; and the door was shut.*

11 *Later the other virgins also came and said, Lord, Lord, open [the door] to us!* **12** *But He replied, I solemnly declare to you, I do not know you [I am not acquainted with you].* **13** *Watch therefore [give strict* *attention and be cautious and active], for you know neither the day nor the hour when the Son of Man will come.*

Now let's quickly examine this passage of scripture, the first wise five virgins were concerned about the things of God. They focus on the kingdom of God. They made sure that their lamps stayed lit with oil.

They did not turn to the cares of this world in all the things that could have been given to them. These virgins were happy being Jesus Bride, they were looking forward to living a life pleasing to Him and to hear Him say Well Done! My good and faithful servants. These wise virgins didn't care how they looked, they only wanted to please their groom (Jesus).

Now the five foolish ones were concerned about the world. These virgins were sleep, literally asleep. What the world thinks of them, what they can gain, and how can they make others like them. What happened? They lost focus on what matters. They were dipping and dapping into the cares and conformity of this world, they fell asleep on the job of ministry. They were so convinced or deceived by the enemy that you must look good and please yourself. It's okay! You only have one life! False! There is a life after this! Let's focus on our eternal estate instead of the physical one.

Psalm 24:3-4 AMP

"Who shall ascend into the hill of the Lord? Or who shall stand in his holy place?

4 He that hath clean hands, and a pure heart, who hath not lifted his soul unto vanity, nor sworn deceitfully.

Now looking at this scripture it is asking us two questions? Followed by two answers: clean hands, and a pure heart. Who has not lifted his soul unto vanity, nor sworn deceitfully? Let's look up clean hands, (blameless, free from dirt, unsoiled.) Pure heart is (clear from blemishes, without any discordant quality, clear and true.)

Now, what is vanity? (Excessive pride in one's appearance,

qualities, abilities, achievements, etc.: character or quality of being vain, conceit:)

(The word sworn is avowed), affirmed, or taking an oath. (Deceitfully is intended to deceive, misleading and fraudulent a deceitful action.) As we can see, these things can be in our hearts, and allow us to stay away from our God. We must be aware that we have a real enemy whose main mission is to blind us and deceive us into going after the things of this world.

Job 15:31 AMP

"Let not him that is deceived trust in vanity; for vanity shall be his recompense. Please my sisters, don't be deceived by the spirit of vanity, its mission is to take you away into captivity to the pride and lust of this world. It's to keep you unclean and defile, and having your garments stained. It travels with a strong illusion of this world's way of doing things. Don't be deceived, come out of her. She has been deceiving for thousands of years with women and men. This spirit means you no good, it wants to continue to captivate you to itself. So, if heads are being turned it's for that spirit, not our Lord and Savior.

This verse in 1 John 2:16 KJV *"For all that is in the world—the lust of the eyes, and the pride of life is not the Father but is of the World"* is referring to His daughters lusting after the things of this world. The Lord is saying wake up my Bride, stop committing adultery with vanity. We know that to love the world ways of doing things cancel out our love for God. We are trusting in secular means to affirm ourselves. We are chasing after the wrong beauty. We are being entice with all sorts of things that brings our attention more to our image than the image God has given to us. Think about it! If you are applying the things of the world rather the things of God you make it an idol. Everything we do has a spirit attached to it. We are accustomed giving our time, attention, and money to the things of this world instead of the things of God. Our investment is in the wrong things. If we are lovers of the world it will allow us the prestige and status and honor that we seek. We will get our rewards from the world that we love so much.

Why do we think idols are things that are made out of carve wood? An idol is anything that you put more interest in more than God. We may not bow to it or pray to our body enhancements, but we do bow to the world system of beauty. Somehow, we sell ourselves to the false beauty in exchange for the real beauty. The false beauty is noting but ashes, and dust at the end our life span.

Israel exchange her spiritual beauty the beauty of idolatrous world. The Prophet Ezekiel declared" "As for the beauty of his ornaments, he set it in majesty; but they made from it the images of their abominations Ezekiel 7:20. We may not be in chains to a dictator, but we are enslaved to the image of this world, rather a surrendered heart towards the cross of Christ.

Have we ever considered asking ourselves; do we invest in ourselves more than God's Kingdom? We can't embody God's beauty if we are constant after the world beauty. The Father knows our heart more than we know it, He knows that our lips say one thing, but our actions is speaking another pursuit in the things of this world. What are we saying to our temple that the Lord resides in? Are we throwing insults at it, when it does not look the way we want it too? Have we been so distorted in our view of beauty that we are our very worst critic? So how do we expect someone to see what we apparently are unable to see. *1 Corinthians3:17*

God say "if anyone defiles the temple of God, God will destroy him. For the temple of God is holy, which temple are you?"

We must know that we have a satisfaction problem, our problem is the lust of the eyes, which stems from having a strong desire of outward things. We live in a world full of superficial. When we eat of the fruit of satisfaction, it gives us a false reality of our real beauty. When we decide to mold our selves in the world view of beauty, it takes away from us the true vessel of honor that we are suppose to be for the Lord. We live in a culture that craves for adorations and compliment of the way our bodies are enhanced. We as God's daughter has gotten the message wrong; we are supposed to reflect Him for others to see His kingdom through us. We must realize that believing the beauty of this world is to empower us, but in reality, it takes our heart away for the one who really cares. It brings us to a place of real emptiness.

Revelation 18:4 AMP

"I heard another voice from heaven, saying, come out of her, my people, that you be not partakers of her sins, and that you receive not of her plagues. 5 for her sins have reached unto heaven, and God hath remembered her iniquities.

It is truly inconceivable that a child of God could be a part of the religious Babylon through elements that may creep in through the world of materialism. These things must be avoided. It is not so much what the world thinks of you or how you look, but it is based on the assignment in which the Lord Himself has called you into. Again, this topic is controversy, this verse is telling us to come out of it. This is truly a warning, for those who are positioned in the Lord as His child, to depart from a place that will lead to destruction. Get out of her ways. Cling closer to Jesus, and the Will of the Father.

The Father is asking "How long will my beloved, continue to stay in bondage of the delusion of the world with its sin and materialism? What will can our answer be towards that answer? It is our duty to present our bodies a living sacrifice unto God which is our reasonable service. We are also told not to be conform to this world; but be transform by the renewing of our minds, to prove what is good, acceptable, and perfect will of God. (Romans 12:1-2 KJV) We truly have a choice to be free or in bondage. We choose! The Bible tells us that who live according to the flesh set their minds on the things of the flesh. *But those who live according to the Spirit will mind the things of the spirit. For to be carnally minded is death; but to be spiritually minded is life and peace. (Romans 8:5-6 KJV)*

Our precious loving Father, wants us to know that we were

brought with a price; that price was the precious blood of Jesus. *1Corinthians 6:19-20* KJV *"What? know that your body is the temple of the Holy Spirit Which is in you, which you have of God, and you are not your own? For ye are bought with a price; therefore, glorify God in your body, and in your spirit, which are God's."*

We must remember that the world is an enemy against God according to James 4:4 KJV and it states "ye adulterers and adulteresses, know ye not that the friendship of the world is enmity(hostility, hatred, ill will, animosity, antagonism) with God? Whosoever therefore will be a friend of the world is the enemy of God. The adulteress is those who revolt for Him. they are lovers of sin, and their acts are those of adulterous women. God is the Lord and husband of every soul that's His. Jesus states in *Matthew 12:30* KJV *"he that is not with Me is against Me".* we are in a covenant relationship with the Lord; therefore, we are to continue in His ways and Will for this life He has given to each one of us.

Psalm 119:37 KJV

***37** Turn away my eyes from beholding vanity (idols and idolatry); and restore me to vigorous life and health in Your ways.*

Let's turn our eyes away from beholding vanity, it is empty. It has no true value to our temporal life. The Lord wants us to turn away and be restore by His eternal love. He wants us to take our eyes out of the mirror, and look more at Him through the Word of God. The Lord tells us that He will give us beauty for ashes (Isaiah 61:3 KJV)

It's truly time to turn from this spirit of vanity, we must know that in everything that we do there is a spirit attached, because you don't see it! doesn't mean that it's not there. Let's be perfectly clear, Jesus was not concerned about His physical appearance, it was all about the will of the Father. This is not a religious point of view, it's a biblical view.

When we give beauty of the world a second look, and create a more beauty in our identity in Christ. If we refuse the world beauty, and accept the kingdom beauty, it will allow us to be refreshing and flourishing in the beauty of the eyes of our King. Our change begins, when we desire Him more than our very existence.

This life, we are to be disciples and make disciples for Christ.

I have prayed about this topic, and I pray that God will reveal to you, your true purpose for Him. It's time for God's Precious Daughters to get back to His Heart. My prayer is that the Holy Spirit of God will reveal to you what is needed for Him to clean you and beautify you from the inside out. I pray that you will begin to see yourself the way He sees you. Love Him and Love you, so you can love others.

This book is to encourage my sisters of faith, and any other sister in the world the importance of loving themselves in a biblical way. It's to encourage them to see themselves as Jesus sees them. The Eternal life has more value than the physical life we live on earth. This Book is to show you ways that you can embrace yourself and see yourself as the Father sees you. Psalms 139:14 KJV] *14 I will praise thee; for I am fearfully [and] wonderfully made: marvelous [are] thy works; and [that] my soul knoweth right well.* Let this book encourage you to have a hunger and thirst for the things of the kingdom. Let your heart be more for the beauty of the Kingdom and focus on our earthly assignments to please our heavenly Father. May the blessings of God be with you as you continue your journey in Him. As the author of this book, my whole desire is that you will receive the adornments within, and see yourself the way that the Father does. My prayer is that you will not allow the world to sway you away from the things of God. My prayer is that the Lord will give you the wisdom, strength and virtue to overcome this spirit of vanity. Prayerfully, you will see your very own reflection in Him your Creator. God bless! Much Kingdom Love, Blessings and Shalom

About the Author

Jacqueline L. Greene, is a Senior Leader along with her husband Walter Greene, at Living The Word Kingdom Church, Hampton VA. I have been commissioned to share the heart of the Father in this end time. I've been ordained and graced to share what the Father is saying to His bride.

I am married to Walter Greene Jr. and we have in our union, two sons, Parrish and Walter Greene III. Also, fourteen grandchildren.

My mission in this book is to cultivate the hearts of women to the heart of the Father. Give them the opportunity to know what our Heavenly Father expects in our intimate relationship with Jesus Christ.

This book will give you the knowledge you need to come out of the conformity of this world concerning your image and be transformed by the renewing of your mind concerning your real identity in Jesus. It is also, to allow you to see your true beauty in the eyes of your Father. It is to show you how much you are beautiful in the eyes of your creator. This book was given to me, after the Lord Himself took me through a stripping of my conformity to this World of beauty. I am so grateful that the Holy Spirit inspired me to write this book in this season.

I pray that this book will be a blessing to you as you continue your journey of life. Hopefully, this book will give you an understanding of your true beauty in God's Word.

I dedicate this book first and foremost to my Heavenly Father, to my family, and my LTWKC family. Also, in loving memory of my deceased grandparents, Clarence & Eula Acker, who raised me and helped me to be the person I am today.

Jacqueline Greene
        C/O
Living The Word Kingdom Church
2816 Build America Dr.
Hampton, VA.23666
email address: livingthewordkingdomchurch@gmail.com
Website: https://www.livingthewordkingdomchurch.com
(757) 827-0694 or (757) 243-3051

Printed in the United States
By Bookmasters